Whole Language Evaluation

Reading, Writing and Spelling

By Jill Eggleton

Contents

FOREWORD

WHOLE LANGUAGE EVALUATION has grown out of the need to develop approaches to evaluation that are in harmony with what we currently know about language learning and teaching.

The present movement toward adopting a "whole-language" philosophy to guide classroom practice can lead to a widening gap between the methods and materials used by teachers to help children learn most effectively and the methods used to evaluate that learning.

WHOLE LANGUAGE EVALUATION is an attempt to bridge that gap.

Teachers may have changed their views on such things as the usefulness of readiness tests, phonics drills, workbook exercises on isolated skills, and even on basal programs. They may also realize that tests and testing affect not only children but also the teachers who use them. But these teachers are also realizing that the changes they wish to make to teaching and learning in their classrooms cannot occur without changing the conceptions of evaluation that exist at present.

WHOLE LANGUAGE EVALUATION will help teachers develop individual achievement. The focus of evaluation is on individual learning—on what each child knows. Every child knows many different things about literacy, but each will start at different points. The implications of this are that children will need the opportunity to learn independently. They will make progress in different ways and have their learning evaluated individually.

The evaluation procedures suggested in this book do not compare one child with another. Any comparisons made are on an individual basis, comparing what a child can do now with what he or she could do before. No evaluation procedure should be used to find, and to define, "winners and losers." The purpose of evaluation should be to find out the things children can nearly do and help them move from being partially successful to being completely successful.

WHOLE LANGUAGE EVALUATION will help teachers to find out each child's strengths and plan future learning based on that information. This implies that evaluation is continuous and is never thought of as an end in itself. All the evaluation procedures suggested in this book are integral and natural parts of the reading and writing program.

We cannot assume that giving tests will, of itself, improve teaching and learning. What teachers—and parents and children—are looking for is what to do to change the results individuals get on tests. Test scores cannot give guidance about both where a child is and what a child needs to learn to move somewhere else along the developmental path.

Because test scores give no idea of the processes that contribute to better learning, teachers have to guess at the reasons for a particular result — and their reasons could be wrong and unfair. For example, tests at the beginning stages of learning rarely measure a child's competence effectively. At these stages, evaluation of learning by observation and monitoring what individual children can do will give more valid information and feedback (to teachers and children) than any test can do.

WHOLE LANGUAGE EVALUATION will help teachers involve children in the evaluation process. In classrooms where learning and teaching are based on a whole-language philosophy, children are responsible for much of their own learning—and consequently their own evaluation. As children read and write (and learn to read by reading, and write by writing) they get the sort of feedback they need to read and write better. They learn a "self-improving system", which means that they learn more about reading every time they read—and more about writing every time they write. The procedures suggested in this book get away from the idea that everything a child learns has been, or must be, taught. Some children can and do teach themselves to read, but many more could, given methods and materials and evaluation procedures that supported the learning they were trying to do.

WHOLE LANGUAGE EVALUATION will help teachers build children's self-esteem. Probably nothing defeats learning more than failing a test, and then being assigned to the lowest group to be "fixed up" (especially if this becomes a cycle of failure, repeated year by year). Constantly comparing children's progress with each other, rather than focusing on individual strengths, is counter productive for children who are less competent. It can be positively dangerous when the deficiencies are equated with difference.

WHOLE LANGUAGE EVALUATION will help teachers gain a balanced view of individual learning. There is no one test that can provide all the information needed to really know what a child can do. A variety of evaluation procedures need to be used to assess individual learning fully.

WHOLE LANGUAGE EVALUATION suggests that the most effective ways teachers can use to find out what children really do know about reading and writing are:

— Listening to children read individually and recording their responses in a systematic way. (See *Running Records* section.)
— Systematic observations of children as they read (and write). (See observation checklists.)
— Noting the creative and constructive responses children make to language learning and keeping records of them. (See *anecdotal records*.)
— Building an individual profile–a *cumulative record* of progress over time. (See *cumulative record card*).
— Talking with and listening to parents.

WHOLE LANGUAGE EVALUATION will provide teachers, children, and their parents with valid information about the progress made in language learning, while also providing the information needed to ensure that each child learns as successfully as possible.

Brian Cutting

Introduction

Monitoring and Evaluation are important parts of teaching and learning.

Monitoring involves the collecting and recording of information in many different ways—both formally and informally—by listening to children read, observing children as they read, collecting samples of work, using appropriate checklists, and having discussions with parents.

Evaluation involves analyzing the data gathered and suggesting strategies for improvement.

Evaluation should be used in conjunction with monitoring to let the children know their achievements — thereby helping them to be as responsible for their own improvement as possible.

The monitoring and evaluation process also helps teachers to choose the materials that will lead to self-improvement and that will help children to read as successfully as possible.

Monitoring: The checking or keeping of a continuous record.	**Evaluation: The analysis of the data gathered.**
Monitoring should be:	Evaluation should be:
<ul><li>Ongoing.</li><li>An integral part of the class program.</li><li>An important part of teaching because a teacher is able to:</li></ul><ul><li>— Find out where the child is at.</li><li>— Learn what the child already knows.</li><li>— Find out what the child needs to know next.</li><li>— Match learning experiences to individuals or groups.</li><li>— Select the right materials.</li><li>— Organise the class program to the best advantage for individual children.</li></ul>	<ul><li>Ongoing, accurate, and objective.</li><li>Concerned with specifics and not generalities.</li><li>Based on the results of careful and thoughtful monitoring.</li><li>Concerned with the child's own analysis of progress—self-evaluation.</li><li>An important part of teaching because a teacher is able to:</li></ul><ul><li>— Gauge the effectiveness of the program in action.</li><li>— Judge the effectiveness of teaching strategies used.</li><li>— Use this information to help plan more effectively.</li></ul>

This book provides a practical guide for the monitoring and evaluation of reading and writing programs for children (approximately five to seven years of age) in their early years of instruction.

Reading

Overview of the Instructional Year

We begin by:—

— Establishing where the child is at.
— Having a plan that caters for that child.
— Having resources so that the plan can be implemented effectively.

For all levels in reading, an overview is established.

(Note: This overview [or plan] would cater for most children between the ages of five and seven. It must be emphasized that it is not the age that determines where to begin but *where the child is at*.)

The overview consists of four parts:

• The teacher's targets: aims or objectives.

• The method: the program used to reach the teacher's targets.

• The children's targets: what the child should achieve at that level.

• Monitoring: the checks and records that are kept in order to determine whether the child has reached the targets.

The overview for reading is divided into three stages* throughout:

Emergent
Early
Fluency

Emergent means: The child is beginning to learn that a book tells a story.

Early means: The child is becoming a reader — i.e., the child is learning to read for meaning.

Fluency means: The child is reading independently — i.e., confidence and competence are increasing.

Note: The concept of stages of development—Emergent, Early, and Fluency—has been used throughout the book as a guide to teachers observing individual learning in language.

* See features of each stage in *Getting Started in Whole Language* by Brian Cutting.

Overview of Reading Program
Emergent Stage

Teacher's Targets and Method		Children's Targets	Monitoring
To establish an interesting, balanced, and enjoyable program:	By Shared Reading, Guided Reading, independent reading, poetry reading, news book, language experience, reading to children, "buddy" reading, reading-related learning centers, home reading, by supplying a wide range of materials that children can read.	To be able to demonstrate front, back, and spine of book.	Entry survey.
		To have correct directional movement.	Observations.
		To have one-to-one correspondence.	
To create a love of reading:	By an enthusiastic approach and showing children that you value reading.	To be able to demonstrate first and last part of story.	Daily individual reading.
To develop an understanding that reading for meaning is paramount:	By discussing stories and pictures in depth, by encouraging children to predict by asking 'why', 'when' and 'where' questions.	To be able to recognize capital letter and lowercase correspondence.	Emergent check.
		To be able to show one letter in a word.	Regular running records.
To give children strategies to increase competence:	By introducing children to the "What can you do when you don't know a word" chart and reinforcing this in all reading experiences.	To show a capital letter.	1 month, 6 month, 1 year entry cumulative record cards.
To develop a vocabulary to use in oral and written language:	By listening to stories, discussing new vocabulary, retelling, role playing, by providing many varied first-hand experiences, by allowing opportunities for interaction.	To recognize the difference between a letter and a word.	
		To be able to recognize some heavy-duty words.	
To establish a program that caters to individual needs:	By ensuring each child's reading is heard daily, by taking regular running records, by flexible groupings.	To recognize similarities in words.	Diagnostic survey (after 1 year).
To give children time to read:	By having a timetable that allows time to read, by providing individual reading boxes, learning centers (reading-related), and allowing opportunities for "buddy" time, reading to parents, and other adults.	To be able to listen to stories.	

Overview of Reading Program
Early Stage

Teacher's Targets and Method		Children's Targets	Monitoring
To establish an interesting, balanced, and enjoyable program:	By Shared Reading, Guided Reading, independent reading, poetry reading, news book, language experience, reading to children, "buddy" reading, reading-related learning centers, home reading, by supplying a wide range of materials that children can read.	To sit for a while and read. / To use meaning as a cue. / To take risks in reading.	Entry Survey. / Observations. / Daily individual reading.
To create a love of reading:	By an enthusiastic approach and showing children that you value reading.	To read on to gain meaning.	Regular running records.
To develop an understanding that reading for meaning is paramount:	By discussing stories and pictures in depth, by encouraging children to predict by asking 'why', 'when' and 'where' questions.	To use text and pictures to sample, predict, and confirm.	1 month, 6 month, 1 year entry on cumulative record cards.
To give children strategies to increase competence:	By reinforcing the "What can you do when you don't know a word" chart in all reading experiences	To self-correct. / To integrate strategies and cross check cue sources.	Diagnostic survey (after 1 year).
To develop a vocabulary to use in oral and written language:	By listening to stories, discussing new vocabulary, retelling, role playing, by providing many varied first hand experiences, by allowing opportunities for interaction.	To be able to retell stories.	
To establish a program that caters to individual needs:	By ensuring each child's reading is heard daily, by taking regular running records, by flexible groupings.		
To give children time to read:	By having a timetable that allows time to read, independently, by providing individual reading boxes, learning centers (reading-related), and allowing opportunities for "buddy" time, reading to parents, and other adults.		

Overview of Reading Program
Fluency Stage

Teacher's Targets and Method		Children's Targets	Monitoring
To establish an interesting, balanced, and enjoyable program:	By Shared Reading, Guided Reading: independent reading, poetry reading, news book, language experience, reading to children, "buddy" reading, reading-related learning centers, home reading, by supplying a wide range of materals that children can read.	To be an independent reader.	Observations.
To create a love of reading:	By an enthusiastic approach and showing children that you value reading.	To be able to read silently.	Running records.
To develop an understanding that reading for meaning is paramount:	By discussing stories and pictures in depth, by encouraging children to predict by asking 'why', 'when' and 'where' questions.	To be able to read with expression.	Reading checklists.
To give children strategies to increase competence:	By reinforcing the "What can you do when you don't know a word" chart.	To be able to differentiate between fiction and nonfiction.	Cumulative record card.
To develop a vocabulary to use in oral and written language:	By listening to stories, discussing new vocabulary, retelling, role playing, by providing many varied first hand experiences, by allowing opportunities for interaction.	To be able to choose suitable reading material.	
To establish a program that caters to individual needs:	By taking regular running records, by flexible groupings, by providing a variety of reading materials for individuals.		
To give children time to read:	By having a timetable that allows time for independent reading, by providing individual reading material, learning centers (reading-related), and allowing opportunities for "buddy" time, reading to parents, and other adults.		

Teachers' Targets —
Methods for Achieving the Targets

(Ref: Sunshine in the Classroom by Brian Cutting.)

"No *one* method of teaching reading will suit all children. It is important that teachers use a variety of approaches."

Shared Reading:
   Shared Reading is reading *with* children. First, a story is read, and a message is given and clarified where necessary. Then, on a rereading, children match their remembered message with text they can see. Books at the Emergent level can be introduced using Shared Reading. Again, the remembered message is matched to a familiar text.

**Sunshine Books for Shared Reading:
Emergent-Early Level:**
The Dippy Dinner Drippers
I'm Glad to Say
Clyde Klutter's Room
The Wicked Pirates
Birthdays
The Little Yellow Chicken
Superkids
Mrs. Muddle Mud-puddle

**Sunshine Books for Shared Reading:
Early-Fluency Level:**
My Wonderful Aunt Stories (1- 6)
A Wizard Came to Visit
The Wizard and the Rainbow

Guided Reading

   Guided Reading is the teacher and a group of children, or an individual child, talking, reading and thinking their way through a text. Reading is often silent which gives children the opportunity to overcome any difficulties without embarrassment. It also encourages self-reliance and helps children to realize what reading is: i.e., that reading is personal contact with an author and not just reading words to someone else - or being read to by someone else. Guided Reading is a supportive bridge between Shared and Independent reading.

Sunshine Books for Shared, Guided, and Independent Reading

Emergent level:

The Airplane	At School
The Barbeque	Baseball
The Birthday Party	Books
Bubbles	Building with Blocks
Come On!	Dressing Up
Faces	The Farm
Getting Dressed	Give Me a Hug
The Great Enormous Hamburger	Our Grandad
I Go, Go, Go	I Am ...
I Write	I Like ...
Look...!	Just Look at You!
My Family	The Merry-go-round
My Home	My Friend
Run!	My Shadow
The Space Ark	Shopping
The Storm	Space Journey
What's in This Egg?	To School
Where's Tim?	What's That?
Baby Gets Dressed	I Love My Family
Huggles' Breakfast	Buzzing Flies
Huggles Can Juggle	Uncle Buncle's House
The Birthday Cake	My Home
Huggles Goes Away	Big and Little
Dinner!	I Am a Bookworm
Down to Town	When Itchy Witchy Sneezes...
I Can Fly	Shoo!
Snap!	The Race
Major Jump	Ice Cream
Little Brother	Our Street
The Long, Long Tail	I Can Jump
What Is a Huggles?	A Hug Is Warm
My Puppy	"Scat!" Said the Cat
Yuk Soup	Shark in a Sack
Our Granny	Up in a Tree

Sunshine Books for Shared, Guided, and Independent Reading

Early level:

Spider, Spider	Bread
Let's Have a Swim!	The Seed
Wake up, Mom!	The Wind Blows Strong
Mr. Grump	Goodbye Lucy
I'm Bigger Than You!	Along Comes Jake
Good for You	Where Are You Going, Aja Rose?
What Would You Like?	
The Monkey Bridge	Come for a Swim
When Dad Went to Playschool	Don't You Laugh at Me!
	My Boat
Letters for Mr James	The Cooking Pot
Mrs. Grindy's Shoes	Little Car
Mishi-na	Noise
Just This Once	Dad's Headache
Mom's Birthday	The Terrible Tiger
Quack, Quack, Quack!	Old Grizzly
Boggywooga	One Thousand Currant Buns
The Giant's Boy	
Nowhere and Nothing	My Sloppy Tiger Goes to School
The Poor Sore Paw	
Mr. Whisper	Boring Old Bed
Ratty-Tatty	Space Race
Red Socks and Yellow Socks	Tess and Paddy
	The Ha-ha Party
The Tiny Woman's Coat	Mom's Diet
My Sloppy Tiger	A Hundred Hugs
The Secret of Spooky House	

Sunshine Nonfiction Books for Shared, Guided, and Independent Reading

Emergent Level:

It Takes Time to Grow	What Am I?
A Small World	Dinosaurs
What Else?	Space
Alien at the Zoo	The Dandelion
The Hermit Crab	Underwater Journey
Are You a Ladybug?	Whose Eggs Are These?
I Wonder	Reading Is Everywhere
Together	Wheels
Clouds	Dreams
The New Building	Building Things
The Tree	Captain B's Boat
Math Is Everywhere	Sunshine Street

Sunshine Books for Guided Reading

Fluency Level

The Train Ride Story	The Giant Pumpkin
Road Robber	Soup
Trash!	Grizzly and the Bumble-
Bogle's Card	bee
Mr. Fixit	Christmas Dog
The Person	Silly Billys
from Planet X	Bogle's Feet
My Sloppy Tiger and	Sloppy Tiger Bedtime
the Party	A Magician's House
The Big Family	In the Middle of the
Dragon with a Cold	Night
Jim's Trumpet	The Manly Ferry Pigeon
The Royal Baby-sitters	When the Cookernup
	Store Burned Down
The Fantastic Washing	The Wedding
Machine	The Trouble with
The Pop Group	Heathrow
Baby's Breakfast	The Man Who Enjoyed
The Garden Party	Grumbling
The Tree Doctor	Feeling Funny
Muppy's Ball	Morning Bath
Jojo and the Robot	Bunrakkit
The New Car	The Old Woman's Nose
Busy Baby	Seasons
The Man Who Never	Lost Property
Told the Truth	Crocodile! Crocodile!
A Lion Song	Anak the Brave
The Little Kite	The Wonderhair Hair
	Restorer

Sunshine Nonfiction Books for Shared, Guided, and Independent Reading.

Early/Fluency level:

It's Not The Same	Double Trouble
Whose Shoes?	Volcanoes
Blackbirds	Animal Pets
The Panda	Did You Know?
The Bug Bus	Robot-a-cise
Time's Up	Seeds
Going to be ...a Butterfly	The Waterhole
The Bone Museum	Grandfather's Ghost
Animals and Air	The Number Cruncher
A Rocket Surprise	Wonders of the World
Rain, Rivers, and Rain	You Are Special
Again	Moving Things
The Humpback Whale	Joy Cowley Writes
The Emperor Penguin	Knights in Armor
No Place Like Home	The Sea Otter
The Solar System	Chicken Dinner
The Super Body Fun Fair	

Independent Reading

Readers read independently at their own pace.

At the Emergent level, children have an individual box or a group box of books that contain "seen" texts—in other words, books that have been introduced to the children.

At the Early level, books in the book boxes are a mixture of seen and unseen texts.

At the Fluency level, books in the book boxes are usually unseen texts (but children may still want to read and reread favorite stories and that is encouraged).

Language Experience

This approach uses the language experiences that children have and the language used by children to write wall stories and class-made books. The children's own experiences are the basis for talking, writing and reading. The texts, written by individuals, groups or the class together with the teacher, are predictable because the experience is shared and the children themselves are the authors (even though the vocabulary is not controlled in any way).

Poetry Reading

A focus poem is introduced each week, and poetry is given a special place in the classroom.

The focus poem is treated in a similar way to a shared book. Favorite poems are read and reread.

The focus poem of the week is pasted into each child's individual poetry book.
A poetry center is established, where children can go to read poems.

Sunshine Books for Focus Poems

Emergent to Early Level:

Now I Am Five
I Dream
Now I Am Six
Changing Days

Sunshine Books for Focus Poems

Early to Fluency Level:

You Are Special
A Different World

Reading to Children

Read stories, poems—the best of literature available—to children. Generally, all such literature will be beyond the children's reading level.

"Buddy" or Paired Reading

Children read to each other or to older children.

Reading-related Learning Centers

At reading time, children may choose to read in established centers, e.g.:
- A reading center—a mini library.
- A poetry center. (A poetry center has a variety of poetry books, nursery rhymes, chants, and poems on cards of varying sizes.)
- Reading around the room—reading the walls. (Using the room as a center.)
- An alphabet center—a variety of alphabet activities.
- A topic book center—a variety of books related to the current theme.
- An overhead projector center—reading transparencies of poems, songs, and children's stories.
- Listening post—listening to and reading taped stories.

- Box of nonfiction reading material
- Shared books and class innovative stories
- Individual published stories

News Book

Interesting articles of news are recorded in a Class News Book and read as a Shared Reading experience. The complexity of the recorded news will depend on the level the children are at. News articles can arise from personal news, newspaper articles, nature finds—anything of personal interest to the children.

Home Reading

Children at the Emergent-Early level can take home:

1. The book they were introduced to at the Guided Reading session (read *to* parents).
2. A library book (read *by* parents).
3. The focus poem (read *with* parents).

Children at the Early-Fluency level can take home:

1. A favorite book (to read independently).
2. A self-selected library book (to read independently).
3. A teacher-chosen story.
4. A library book (for parents to read *to* or *with* their children).
5. The focus poem.

Independent Reading

Children learn to read—and read better—by reading. A wide range of fiction and nonfiction books is needed, if children are to learn.

Children's Targets

The following Targets Chart outlines the skills that children should have at each of the Emergent-Fluency reading levels. They are skills taught and reinforced through the "method" as indicated in the overview.

In all reading and writing activities, opportunity should be taken to introduce or reinforce these targets. It is not intended that they be taught in isolation.

Emergent Level

Children's Target:

— to be able to demonstrate front, back, and spine of book.
— to have correct directional movement
— to have one-to-one correspondence.
— to be able to demonstrate first and last part of story.
— to be able to recognize capital letter and lowercase correspondence.
— to be able to show one letter in a word.
— to show a capital letter.
— to recognize the difference between a letter and a word.
— to be able to recognize some heavy-duty, or high frequency, words.
— to recognize similarities in words.
— to be able to listen to stories.

Early Level

Children's Target:

— to sit for a while and read.
— to use meaning as a cue.
— to take risks in reading.
— to read on to gain meaning.
— to use texts and pictures to sample, predict, and confirm.
— to self-correct.
— to integrate strategies and cross check cue sources.
— to be able to retell stories.

Fluency Level

Children's Target:

— to be an independent reader
— to be able to read silently.
— to be able to read with expression.
— to be able to differentiate between fiction and nonfiction.
— to be able to choose suitable reading material.

Individual Files in Reading and Writing:

An individual file is established for each child on his entry to school. The individual file contains:

Name, age, date of birth, date of entry to school.
Preschool experiences.
Parent or guardian.
Health/welfare factors.

Permanent Data for First Three years:

— Reading checklists.
— Written language/spelling development checklists.
— Monthly running record sheet.
— Entry survey.
— Written language samples.
— Handwriting samples.
— Observation notes.
— Parent interview notes.

Non-Permanent Data (Not Necessary to Retain after Completion)
Emergent check.
Alphabet checks.
Running record forms (information transferred to monthly running record sheet).

Permanent Data (To Be Retained for Child's Schooling)
Cumulative record card.

Monitoring Progress

Monitoring is finding out what the child already knows and where to lead him to next.

In reading, the following methods are used to monitor the three levels:

Emergent Level Monitoring	Early Level Monitoring	Fluency Level Monitoring
Entry Survey	Entry Survey	Observations
Observations	Observations	Running records
Daily individual reading	Daily individual reading	Reading checklists
Emergent check Reading checklists	Emergent check Reading checklists	Cumulative record card entries
Running records	Running records	Self-evaluation
1 month, 6 month, 1 year entry cumulative record cards.	1 month, 6 month, 1 year entry cumulative record cards	
Diagnostic survey (after 1 year)	Diagnostic survey (after 1 year)	
Self-evaluation	Self-evaluation	

Entry Survey

This survey is usually completed at the end of the child's first week at school. It is helpful in giving the teacher a quick overview of some skills a child may have on entering school.

It is filed in the "individual file", but it must be kept in mind that it is an Entry Survey and therefore only an initial guide.

Entry Survey

Name .... Date ....

Oral Language:
E.S.L.
Confident
Responds to questions

Reading:
Listens to stories
Has correct directional movement
Can match one-to-one
Can read competently

Written Language:
Level
Eager to write

Spelling:
Stage
Has knowledge of letter names
Has knowledge of letter sounds
Can write name
Drawing sample:

Comment if necessary
Health:

Physical/social development:

Parent concerns and expectations

General observations:

Observations of Reading

As teachers, it is very important to take time to observe children in as many different situations as possible. Specific notes need to be kept when these observations are made.

In terms of reading, the following are some behaviors to monitor by general observations. More specific and detailed observations would be made by taking a running record or by listening to children read daily.

Emergent-Early

1. Is the child able to listen to a story?
2. Is the child able to retell a story?
3. Does the child elect to read/look at books in a "free choice" time?
4. Does the child look for details in pictures?
5. Does the child want to share stories?

Early-Fluency

1. Is the child able to listen to a story?
2. Is the child able to retell a story?
3. Does the child elect to read/look at books in a "free choice" time?
4. Does the child look for details in pictures?
5. Does the child want to share stories?
6. Is the child choosing books that can be read?
7. Is the child visiting the library?
8. Is the child eager to take books home?
9. Is the child selecting a variety of books?

The above points are examples of things to observe. There will be others.

The important initial considerations are attitude and interest.

One of the teacher targets in the overview states "to create a love of reading." If, after observations, there are indications that a child is not "tuned in" to reading, it is the teacher's responsibility to create an interest.

If possible, parents need to be involved. A parent interview should be arranged with the teacher and parent together deciding on how best to help the child.

Suggestions to parents could be:

— Reading daily to the child.
— Visiting the library regularly.
— Pointing out to the child words in the world around him, e.g. signs, lists...

These observational notes can be recorded in a teacher's work plan as in this example:

	DATE & OBSERVATION	TEACHER ACTION
	7/2 Appears to listen well but cannot retell a story with much accuracy. Skims quickly through books without attention to detail.	7/2 Draw attention to picture detail — Discuss in depth — Concentrate on predicting. After reading recap main points — Dramatize.
	12/4 Able to retell simple stories with more accuracy. Still needs to concentrate on picture detail. Unable to predict with confidence.	Encourage her to retell story to peers or other adults.
		12/4 Discussed with parent need for regular bed-time stories. Explained how to talk through a story with Jaime.

It must be noted that as with most data gathering, observations of reading behavior are ongoing.

Running Records

(Ref: Marie Clay - The Early Detection of Reading Difficulties.)

Central to effective monitoring is the technique of taking running records. Because running records describe accurately what actually occurs in the course of reading, they provide the most helpful insights about the strategies a child is using to reconstruct meaning.

Running records can be taken on both seen and unseen texts. Taking running records on a seen text reveals whether the difficulty level of the material that the child has been using is suitable and how well the child makes use of the strategies that have been taught. Using unseen texts reveals the child's willingness to take risks and his or her ability to use and integrate strategies independently.

Running records are taken at least once per month — but more often if there is a need. They are taken as part of the weekly reading program. For example, instead of taking a group of children for a Guided Reading lesson, running records can be taken of individuals in the group.

It is important to analyze each error the child has made. When this is done, the teacher gets a real indication of what the child's strategies in reading are.

Analyze children's reading by using the M.S.V. code. Write M.S.V. on the record form. (M is for meaning, S for structure, and V for visual cues.) Circle the cues the child used on each error or self-correction. The uncircled letters will then show the cues neglected.

A summary of each month's running record is entered on the <u>Monthly Running Record</u> form in the child's individual file.

(Refs: The Early Detection of Reading Difficulties, Marie Clay. Getting Started in Whole Language, Brian Cutting.)

Taking a Running Record

Select a passage/text of 100 to 200 words. (At earliest levels there may be fewer than 100 words.)

1. Check off each correct response.
2. Record every error in full.
3. Calculate the accuracy rate:
$$\frac{E}{100 - RW} \quad \frac{100}{X \quad 1}$$
$$\frac{15}{100 - 100} \quad \frac{100}{X \quad 1} = 85\% \text{ accuracy}$$
4. Calculate the self-correction rate:
$$\frac{E + SC}{SC} \quad \frac{10 + 5}{5} = 1:3$$
5. Ask the child to retell the story. This will give an indication of how well the story is understood.

Note: See the Diagnostic Survey in Marie Clay's *The Early Detection of Reading Difficulties* for complete information on the conventions used in taking a running record.

RUNNING RECORD SUMMARY: SAMPLE

NAME: SCOTT   DATE: 21.7.89   AGE: 5.6

TEXT: One Thousand Currant Buns   LEVEL: Early   ~~SEEN~~/UNSEEN

RUNNING WORDS: 80   ERROR RATE: $\frac{RW}{E}$ 1-13   ACCURACY: 93%

SELF CORRECTIONS: 4   S.C. RATE: $\frac{E + SC}{SC}$ 1 - 2·5

ANALYSIS OF ERRORS:

Cues used: meaning, structure, visual.
Cues neglected: visual, whole word. Using visual for initial and final letters only.

M.	Meaning	3
S.	Structure	3
V.	Visual	3

Comment on Reading:

Scott is using meaning and structure cues. He is rerunning. While he is using some visual cues, he is not looking at the whole word. He needs to cross-check using visual cues.

	ERRORS			S.C.
	M	S	V	
✓✓ ✓✓✓ $\frac{mrs.}{miss}$ E	I	I		
✓✓✓ $\frac{went}{want}$ sc ✓✓✓✓				I
✓✓ ✓✓✓✓ ✓✓ ✓✓✓✓✓ ✓ ✓ rerun				
✓ ✓✓ $\frac{in}{on}$ sc				I
✓✓✓ $\frac{mrs.}{miss}$ E	I	I		
✓✓✓ ✓✓✓✓ ✓ $\frac{sc}{screamed}$ E			I	
✓✓✓✓ rerun				
✓✓✓✓ $\frac{the}{a}$ sc				I
✓ $\frac{bl}{bleated}$ E			I	
✓✓✓ ✓✓✓✓ ✓✓ $\frac{a}{the}$ sc				I
✓ $\frac{yelled}{yelped}$ E	I	I		
✓✓✓ ✓✓✓✓ $\frac{growed}{growled}$ E			I	

24

MONTHLY RUNNING RECORD SHEET

Year: ....   Name: ....

Month	Title	Level	S/US	Accuracy	S.C.	Comment
January						
February	What's in This Egg?	Emergent	S	100%	Nil	One-to-one and left-to-right established. Eager attitude.
March	Yuk Soup	Emergent	S	100%	Nil	Uses picture clues, confident & expressive.
April	Uncle Buncle's House	Emergent	S	100%	Nil	Rerunning. Very capable. Retells story easily. Emergent check needed.
May	The Cooking Pot	Early	US	91%	1.3	Using meaning and structure cues. Reads on to gain meaning. Using some visual cues but beginning sounds only.
June	The Terrible Tiger	Early	US	92%	1.2	Very expressive. Errors made did not affect the meaning, e.g., forest/jungle.
July						
August						
September						
October						
November						
December						

A running record is taken each month. The results are recorded as in the sample sheet above and specific comments are made about the child's reading behavior.
SC: Self-correction. S/US: Seen/Unseen.

Emergent Check

When it is considered that the child may be ready for the Early level of reading, an Emergent Check can be given.

EMERGENT CHECK	
Name .... Date...........................	
1) Can sit for a time and read a book	
2) Can find cover and turn pages correctly	
3) Knows where to start	
4) Has left to right movement	
5) Can identify a word	
6) Can identify a letter	
7) Can match one to one	
8) Can match words that are same, e.g, here, went, this, we, here.	
9) Can write name	
10) Can recognize similarities in words, e.g, me, my, mouse. his, her, he. see, is, stop.	
11) Can guess a caption for a picture, e.g, Here is a house	
12) Can identify some heavy duty words, e.g, Is, here, am, come, I, said, can, look, and, a, my, the, mom, like, go, dad, we, up, to.	

To administer, give children a familiar book and observe reading behavior. Any difficulties experienced may be used as teaching points.

This check is given to check a child's readiness to move to the Early Reading Level. It is filed in the "individual file."

A Reading Checklist

This is a means of checking and recording what the child has attained and where he needs to go to next.

Reading checklists should be taken regularly (at the completion of the monthly running record would seem an appropriate time). The following is an example of a reading checklist.

READING CHECKLIST

Name:

	Date	Comment
Early:		
Willing to take risks		
Uses meaning as a cue		
Uses structure as a cue		
Uses visual cue		
Checks responses using a variety of cues		
Self monitoring - does the child recognize he/she has made an error?		
Self corrects		
Can retell the story		

Fluency:		
Is able to read silently		
Reads with expression		
Is able to select suitable reading material		
Can differentiate between fiction and non fiction		

This Reading Checklist is filled in after taking a monthly running record.

Cumulative Record Card

A cumulative record card is a system of keeping records about each pupil's individual progress. This card provides information that is based on their achievements and is transferred from class to class as the child moves through the school.

It should provide the following information:

— Name, school, date of birth, date entered school, last preschool.
— Preschool experience.
— Health and welfare factors.
— Attendance after one month, one year.
— Observations after first month of school.
— Progress in personal and social development and in curriculum areas. (To be filled in twice per year.)

Each child has a cumulative record card. Entries are made at one month, six months, one year, and thereafter twice per year.

The cumulative reading record card would contain all the specific information gained from the data gathering.

At one month. it would indicate the child's interest in books and stories, eagerness to return to favorite stories and the concepts of print established. (See Reading Checklists.)

• At six months and thereafter, it would indicate level of reading, attitudes, and skills:

— Can the child tell when his or her own reading does not make sense?
— Can the child use a wide range of strategies flexibly and independently and learn from his or her own mistakes?
— Does the child display an interest in books and the ideas in them, returning frequently to favorites?
— Does the child listen appreciatively to stories?
— What level of reading is the child at—Emergent, Early, Fluency?

A Sample Cumulative Record Card

Name: _____
School: _____ Date of birth: _____
Date entered school: _____
Preschool experience: _____
_____
_____
_____

HEALTH FACTORS	WELFARE CONCERNS

FIRST MONTH OBSERVATIONS

_____
_____
_____
_____

6 MONTH ENTRY	1 YEAR ENTRY
Date: _____	Date: _____
Language:	Language:
Oral: _____	Oral: _____
Written: _____	Written: _____
Reading: _____	Reading: _____
Spelling: _____	Spelling: _____
Mathematics: _____	Mathematics: _____
Personal & social development: _____	Personal & social development: _____

Second Year Entry

Language:

Listening/speaking: _____

Reading: _____

Writing: _____

Mathematics: _____

Science: _____

Social studies: _____

Physical education: _____

Health: _____

Art: _____

Music: _____

PERSONAL AND SOCIAL DEVELOPMENT

ATTENDANCE	COMPLETE AT	TEACHER'S SIGNATURE	DATE
	1 month		
	1 year		
	2nd year		
	3rd year		

Daily Individual Reading

At the Emergent and Early stages of reading particularly, it is suggested that the teacher listen daily to each child reading a familiar text.

By listening daily to a child read or by asking a child to retell the story, the teacher has a regular and frequent opportunity to confirm and reinforce appropriate behaviors and thereby ensure that each day the child's reading is being monitored.

This daily rereading of familiar texts at the Emergent and Early stages encourages the child's confidence and fluency.

At the Fluency stage of reading, it is important for the teacher to ask the child questions about a book he or she has read independently. Some questions could be:

— Did you enjoy the story?

— What part did you enjoy the most?

— Read me a page/paragraph/sentence you liked.

— Why do you think ...?

— How do you think ...?

The purpose should be to monitor the child's interest and to ensure that meaning is being gained from the story that he or she is reading independently.

Diagnostic Survey

A Diagnostic Survey is taken after a year's instruction at school. It is taken to ensure that any child having real or potential difficulties is identified as early as possible.

It also provides an opportunity to evaluate the children's learning in the first year of teaching.

The results of the diagnostic survey are shared with parents. If the survey indicates the child is at risk, extra help should be given. This could be in the form of:

1. An individual program.
2. Reading recovery.
3. Peer tutoring.

The diagnostic survey is filed in the child's individual file.

For guidance on how to administer the Diagnostic Survey, see *The Early Detection of Reading Difficulties* (1979) by Marie Clay.

Self-evaluation

Children need to play an active role in evaluation.

Self-evaluation can really only succeed where children have a chance to develop and improve their ideas about how to read by reading books of many kinds.

"Teachers should aim to produce independent readers whose reading improves whenever they read, and who are responsible for monitoring their own reading." — Brian Cutting, *Getting Started in Whole Language.*

Marie Clay states that "effective self-monitoring begins early but must be continually adapted to encompass new challenges in texts."

She advances the following methods to use in the encouragement of self-monitoring at the early stages:

— Ask the child to point (one-to-one matching).
— Direct the child's attention to meaning.
— Say such things as "I liked the way you did that. But can you find the hard bit? Was that all right? Why did you stop? What did you notice? I liked the way you tried to work that out. Check to see if what you read looks right and sounds right."

Questions such as these encourage the children to think about what they are doing when they read. They encourage children to check one kind of cue against another and to solve problems for themselves, and lead them toward independence.

"A successful reader, who is making no errors, is monitoring his reading at all times." — Marie Clay, *The Early Detection of Reading Difficulties.*

At the Fluency stage of reading when the child is fluent and independent, self-evaluation still needs to be encouraged.

The child needs to consider the type of stories he or she prefers to read, and why. Is the child varying his reading material? Does the child spend time on reading? Is he or she able to read aloud to interest an audience?

Encourage children to analyze their own reading and to become aware of how they may be able to improve further by using the following chart:

Introduce this chart as early as possible in a child's reading experience.

Ask the children "what can you do when you don't know a word" and encourage them to verbalize the answer. Reinforce this process as often as possible.

What can you do when you don't know a word?

Go back to the beginning of the sentence.
Read again.
Say the first sound.

If you get stuck again:
Go back to the beginning of the sentence.
Read again.
Say the first sound, then ...
Read on to the end of the sentence.

Now give it a try:
— Does it make sense?
— Does it look right?
— Does it sound right?

Using the Data

The data collected is used in the following ways:

* Evaluating the program.
* Reporting to parents.

Evaluating the Program:

When evaluating the reading program in action, it is important to consider whether or not the teacher targets are being achieved.

— Is the program balanced?
  (A variety of methods and materials are being used.)
— Are the children eager to read?
  (Observation.)
— Do the children demonstrate a real interest in books?
  (Observation.)
— Do they show an understanding of the stories read?
  (Observations, running records.)
— Do any children need regrouping?
  (Running records, Emergent check.)
— Are they using reading strategies?
  (Running records, Daily reading check.)
— Are the individual needs of each child being catered to?
  (Diagnostic survey, entry survey, running records).
— Is there time to practice reading skills independently?

Reporting to Parents

Reports, whether oral or written, should focus upon the learning achievements of the individual child. They should describe the knowledge, skills, attitudes, and values being developed and should be in sufficient detail for the parents to feel confident that the report informs them about the learning that has occurred.

Reporting to parents should be frequent and meaningful. It should be designed to ensure that parents are able to share the very important information that they have about their child's progress and attitudes toward learning with the teachers.

In reporting to parents on reading the following suggestions are made:

1. Outline by newsletter or parent meeting the reading program. This could include the teacher targets and the methods by which the targets intend to be reached.

2. After one month of the school year, arrange a parent/teacher discussion. This is a time for the parents to share information about the child with the teacher. It is important to find out the child's attitude toward reading at home — whether the child is eager to visit the library or what emphasis the parents place on reading in the home. The teacher might share with the parent the observation notes on the entry survey.

   Any relevant information is recorded in the individual file or on the cumulative record card.

3. After approximately five months of the school year, a formal interview between parent and teacher is arranged. This is the time for the teacher to share with the parent the learning achievement of the child.

The teacher will use the data gathered from:

A. Running records. These records will need to be explained to the parents. The teacher will indicate what the child does when he or she is reading.

B. Observation notes. Share with the parent the reading behavior the teacher has observed both in formal and informal situations.

C. Reading checklists. Indicate to the parent the stage that the child is at and where he or she will go to next.

D. Emergent checks. Entry surveys would be shared.

At the conclusion of this interview, the parent should know specifically:

— What the child is able to do in reading.
— What the next step or steps will be.
— What the parent can do to help achieve the next steps.

4. At the conclusion of the school year, a written report is issued to parents. This should contain relevant, specific comments on the individual child's achievements.

It should contain information as to the child's:

— Understanding of reading.
— Skills and knowledge of reading.
— Attitudes in reading.

Sample of a Newsletter to Parents:

Dear Parent,

The staff of (your school name here) welcome you as a parent and look forward to a pleasurable association with you.

We would like to share some positive ways you could help your child in reading and written-language development.

Reading
Set aside a regular time each night to read to your child. The bedtime story is the most valuable way to ensure a healthy attitude toward reading.

Make this time enjoyable and free from tension.

Most nights, your child will bring home a book for you to share together. Listen to your child read. If he or she is at the beginning stages of reading, help him or her to point to the words. Do not isolate letters and sounds. Reading is gaining meaning, not just saying words. Encourage your child to gain sense from the story. Resist jumping in and correcting errors, but ask questions like "Does this make sense? What does it start with?"

Our aim is to create in children a love of books and to lead them toward being independent readers. To do this, we teach them strategies to cope with an unknown word. These strategies appear on a chart labeled "What To Do When You Come to a Word You Don't Know."

This chart is pasted on the child's home reading folder. You can become familiar with this so that you will understand just what your child is attempting to do.

Encourage your child to retell a story in his or her own words.

Words are everywhere. When you go shopping or on outings, read signs and labels.

Each Friday, your child will bring home his or her poetry book. In this is the poem of the week. Let your child share it with you.

Written Language:
In written language, we are encouraging children to become independent writers from the beginning. The children are asked to attempt to write their own stories regardless of their letter or word knowledge. All approximations are accepted and correct letters and words are modeled by the teacher. If your child wants to write at home, first encourage him or her to write independently.

Please do not compare one child with another. They are all individuals and progress at their own rate.

Our aim is to provide a happy, caring environment with each child actively involved in the learning process.

We would be pleased to discuss any problems or queries that you may have concerning your child. The door is always open.

Yours sincerely,

Writing

Overview of the Instructional Year:

We begin by:

— Establishing where the child is at.
— Having a plan that caters to that child.
— Having resources so that the plan can be implemented effectively.

<u>For all levels in writing, an overview is established.</u>

(Note: This overview [or plan] would cater to most children between the ages of five and seven. It must be emphasized that it is not the age that determines where to begin but *where the child is at.*)

The overview consists of four parts:

• The teacher's targets: aims and objectives.

• The method: the program used to reach the teacher's targets.

• The children's targets: what the child should achieve at that level.

• Monitoring: the checks and records that are kept in order to determine whether the child has reached the targets.

<u>The overview for an instructional year in written language is divided into three stages.</u>

Stage 1: Emergent
Stage 2: Early
Stage 3: Fluency

Emergent means: The child is making a start. Scribble, or isolated letters tell a story.

Early means: The child is becoming a writer.

Fluency means: The child is writing independently. Confidence and competence are increasing.

Overview of Writing Program
Emergent Stage

Teacher's Targets and Method		Children's Targets	Monitoring
To establish an interesting, balanced, and enjoyable program:	By Shared Writing, Guided Writing, independent writing, language experiences, writing for children, writing-related learning centers, by exposing children to a variety of writing types.	Process Focus: To have correct directional movement.	Entry Survey. Observations.
		To leave spaces between words.	Skills I am able to do (personal writing books filled in weekly).
To create a love of writing:	By an enthusiastic approach.	To use approximations.	
To encourage children to make approximations:	By encouraging all efforts made, by praising what the child is able to do.	To use approximations according to the sound heard at the beginning of words.	Writing sample 6 times per year for individual files.
To develop a wide vocabulary:	By listening to stories, discussing new vocabulary, retelling, role playing, by providing many varied first hand experiences, by allowing opportunities for pupil/teacher interaction.	To use some heavy-duty words appropriately.	Writing checklists.
To establish a program that caters to individual needs:	By careful monitoring of children's writing progress, by individual conferencing, by avoiding comparisons.	Product Focus: To confidently choose a topic to write on.	1 month, 6 month, 1 year on cumulative record card.
To give children time to write:	By establishing a writing center and a timetable that allows freedom to write.		Diagnostic survey (after 1 year).

Overview of Writing Program
Early Stage

Teacher's Targets and Method		Children's Targets	Monitoring
To establish an interesting, balanced, and enjoyable program:	By Shared Writing, Guided Writing, independent writing, language experiences, writing for children, writing-related learning centers, by exposing children to a variety of writing types.	**Process Focus:** To use approximations. To use beginning and end sounds of words.	Observations. Skills I am able to do (personal writing books filled in weekly).
To create a love of writing:	By an enthusiastic approach.	To use vowels. To spell many heavy-duty words correctly.	
To encourage children to make approximations:	By encouraging all efforts made, by praising what the child is able to do.	To use more correctly spelled words than approximations.	Writing sample 6 times per year for individual files.
To develop a wide vocabulary:	By listening to stories, discussing new vocabulary, retelling, role playing, by providing many varied first hand experiences, by allowing opportunities for pupil/teacher interaction.	To begin using editing skills: to place periods to place capital letters to locate approximations by underlining	Writing checklists.
To establish a program that caters to individual needs:	By careful monitoring of children's writing progress, by individual conferencing, by avoiding comparisons.	to begin to correct approximations by using word sources.	Entry on cumulative record card.
To give children time to write:	By establishing a writing center and a timetable that allows freedom to write.	**Product Focus:** To give an appropriate title for a story. To write on a variety of topics.	

Overview of Writing Program
Fluency Stage

Teacher's Targets and Method		Children's Targets	Monitoring
To establish an interesting, balanced, and enjoyable program:	By Shared Writing, Guided Writing, independent writing, language experiences, writing for children, writing-related learning centers, by exposing children to a variety of writing types.	**Process Focus** To use editing skills: • uses punctuation marks correctly • divide a story into paragraphs • publishes correct articles of work • uses word sources	Observations Skills I am able to do (personal writing books filled in weekly)
To create a love of writing:	By an enthusiastic approach.	**Product Focus**	
To encourage children to make approximations:	By encouraging all efforts made, by praising what the child is able to do.	To vary sentence beginnings	Writing sample 6 times per year for individual files.
To develop a wide vocabulary:	By listening to stories, discussing new vocabulary, retelling, role playing, by providing many varied first hand experiences, by allowing opportunities for pupil/teacher interaction.	To sequence ideas To use a wide vocabulary	Entry on cumulative record card

To establish a program that caters to individual needs:	By careful monitoring of children's writing progress, by individual conferencing, by avoiding comparisons.	To write in a variety of styles
		  friendly letter
		  factual
		  report
		  imaginative
		  retelling
		  poetry
		  fiction
			Writing checklists

To give children time to write:	By establishing a writing center and a timetable that allows freedom to write.		

Teachers' Targets —
Methods for Achieving the Targets

Shared Writing: A group or class activity.

This is writing <u>with</u> children.   Together, the teacher and children construct a sentence, a paragraph, or a story.

Guided Writing: An individual or small-group activity.

This enables the teacher and child to think and talk their way through constructing a sentence, a paragraph, or a story.

<u>A suggested approach is:</u>

1. Deciding on the purpose for writing.
2. Stimulating the child's interest.
3. The teacher begins the story, getting the child to help with words, punctuation, ideas.
4. The child writes part of the story alone with the teacher guiding where appropriate.
5. On completion, the teacher and child share the story together.

Independent Writing:

Children are writing on their own, at their own pace and usually on a self-selected topic.

Have two different folders for each child.

<u>A non-teaching book or folder:</u>

Child writes his or her story in this book. Parent helpers can be trained to model the story underneath and ask the child to read it back.

<u>A teaching book or folder:</u>

Child writes his or her story in this book. The teacher "conferences" with the child on the completion of the story. This is the teaching time. The teacher focuses on a teaching point with each individual child. For example, at the Emergent level, it might be helping the child to use spaces or initial letters. At the Early level, it might be helping the child to use end sounds or periods. At the Fluency level, the teaching point might be helping the child vary sentence beginnings.

This same program can be adapted to suit children at the Fluency level, but more time needs to be given in the teaching book due to the increasing quantity and length of their stories.

Language Experiences:
Making a story using the children's own language and experiences. The text can be written by individuals, group, or the class together.

Writing for Children:
The teacher "models" a sentence, paragraph, story, letter, poem, or list. It is important that the teacher model a variety of writing types. For example:

imaginative writing   letter writing
report writing   diary writing
retelling   list writing
poetry writing

Writing-related Learning Centers:

Writing centers are areas where children can practice writing or writing-related skills.
Incorporate a variety of paper shapes and sizes, pencils, felt pens, colored pencils, alphabet
cards, and chart of ideas for story starters.

Time to Write:
Give children time to write by establishing a writing center and a timetable that allows the
children the freedom to write.

Alphabet center:
Emergent level. Alphabet activities and games are provided.

Dictionary center:
Early - Fluency. A variety of dictionaries, word games, dictionary activities.

Chalkboard center:
Chalks or markers are provided for writing.

Overhead projector center:
Transparencies and markers are provided.

Children's Targets

These are the targets that it is suggested the child should achieve at the Emergent, Early, and Fluency levels of written language.

These skills are taught and reinforced in all reading and writing activities. It is not intended that they be taught in isolation or as written exercises. Shared books, Guided Reading, modeling of children's writing are just some ways children can be exposed to these targets.

It should be noted that these targets have a Process Focus and a Product Focus.

At the Emergent and Early stages of written language, it is important that the children understand the actual process of writing. Once this process is understood, then the product can be given greater consideration. And this extends through the levels.

Emergent Level
Children's Target:

Process Focus
— to have correct directional movement
— to leave spaces between words
— to use approximations
— to use approximations according to the sound heard at the beginning of words
— to use some heavy duty, or high frequency words appropriately

Product Focus
— to confidently choose a topic to write on

Early Level
Children's Target:

Process Focus
— to use approximations
— to use beginning and end sounds of words
— to use vowels
— to spell many heavy duty, or high frequency words correctly
— to use more correctly spelled words than approximations
— to begin using editing skills:
  to place periods
  to place capital letters
  to locate approximations by underlining
  to begin to correct approximations by using word sources

Product Focus
— to give an appropriate title for a story
— to write on a variety of topics

Fluency Level
Children's Target:

Process Focus
— to use editing skills:
  to place quotation marks
  to place question marks
  to place apostrophes
  to place commas
  to divide the story into paragraphs
  to publish correct articles of work

Product Focus
— to vary sentence beginning
— to sequence ideas
— to use a wide vocabulary
— to write in a variety of styles: friendly letter, factual, report, imaginative, retelling, poetry.

Monitoring Progress

This is finding out what the child can do and where to lead the child to next.

In writing, the following methods are used to monitor progress.

Emergent-Early Monitoring
Observations.
"Skills I am able to do" chart (personal writing books—fill in weekly).
Writing sample 6 times per year for individual files.
1 month, 6 month, 1 year on cumulative record card.
Diagnostic Survey.
Writing checklists.
Entry survey.

Fluency Monitoring
Observations
"Skills I am able to do" chart (personal writing books).
Writing sample 6 times per year for individual files.
Entry on cumulative record card.
Writing checklists in individual files.

Entry Survey

This survey is usually completed at the end of the child's first week at school.

It is filed in the "individual file" but it is helpful in giving the teacher a quick overview of some skills a child may have entered school with and determines a starting point in the child's program.

The written-language stage that the child enters school with and whether the child shows interest in writing a story should be noted.

Entry Survey

Name .... Date ....

Oral Language:
E.S.L.
Confident
Responds to questions

Written Language:
Stage
Eager to write

Reading:
Listens to stories
Has correct directional movement
Can match one-to-one
Can read competently

Spelling:
Stage
Has knowledge of letter names
Has knowledge of letter sounds
Can write name
Drawing sample:

Comment if necessary
Health:

Physical/social development:

Parent concerns and expectations

General observations:

Observations of Writing

The important general observations that should be made are those that indicate attitude and interest and specific notes need to be kept on these observations.

The following are examples of writing behavior to observe:

1. Does the child settle quickly to the task of writing?

2. Is the child able to stay "on task" and be involved in the story being written?

3. Does the child elect to write in the free-choice time?

4. Is the child eager to share his or her story with others?

These observational notes can be recorded in a teacher's work plan. For example:

Anecdotal Notes - Observations of Children

NAME	DATE & OBSERVATION	TEACHER ACTION
Sarah	7/2 Has interesting ideas but reluctant to use approximations — wants to be correct.	Arranged interview with parent — Parent not aware of the importance of allowing child to approximate. Use as parent help.
	13/3 Still slow at recording ideas but beginning to use approximations.	Continue to encourage all attempts at approximating words.

More specific and detailed observations concerning the level and needs of the child would appear on the written-language samples and checklists in the child's personal writing folder.

Writing Samples

Approximately six times per year, a written language sample is taken.

It must be noted that this sample is part of the normal weekly written language program. To obtain an accurate sample, a test-like situation must be avoided.

An example of written-language sampling over a year of instruction: Brooke, from age five years to age five years, ten months.

Stage 1:
Emergent
— can write letters.
— has correct directional movement.

Stage 1:
Emergent
— beginning to leave spaces.

Stage 1:
Emergent
— using approximations.
— using beginning sounds.
— using some heavy-duty, or high frequency words.

Stage 2:
Early
— using approximations.
— using beginning and end sounds.
— confidently writing on a topic.

I drm I
Was a dp G
and I Scd
my fSz

I dreamt I was a
dragon and I scared
my friends.

I had a lion
in My house.
I fdi Sdi
felt scared.
my moM Sdt.
screamed.
and the lion
Went A Wy.
away

Stage 2:

Early
— can spell many heavy-duty, or high frequency words.

Stage 2:

Early
— using more correctly spelled words than approximations.
— becoming aware of periods and capital letters.
— writing on a variety of topics.

Writing Checklists

This is a means of checking and recording what the child has attained and where he or she needs to go to next.

Writing checklists should be taken regularly—after a written-language sample would seem an appropriate time.

The following are examples of writing checklists at the Emergent, Early, and Fluency stages of writing.

It must be noted that because spelling forms an integral part of the writing process, the two checklists are "meshed" together.

Record of Written Language and Spelling Development

Spelling Stage 1 Emergent	Written Language Stage 1 Emergent	Date when mastered — Comment if necessary
	Process Focus	
	Pre-letter writing	
	Writing letters	
	Correct directional movement	
	Leaves spaces	
	Uses approximations	
	Uses initial consonants	
Knows letter names and letter sounds		
Uses some known words in correct places		
	Product Focus: Able to select own topic to write on.	

Record of Written Language and Spelling Development

Spelling Stage 2 Early	Written Language Stage 2 Early	Date when mastered — Comment if necessary
Process Focus		
Uses end sounds of most words correctly		
Uses vowels		
Able to spell many heavy-duty words correctly		
Uses more correct spellings than approximations		
Uses initial blends		
Uses editing skills Underlines approximations		
Uses word sources to correct approximations		
	Uses capital letters in correct place	
	Uses periods in correct place	
	Product Focus: Writes a title	
	Varies topic choice	

Record of Written Language and Spelling Development

Spelling Stage 3 Fluency	Written Language Stage 3 Fluency	Date when mastered —Comment if necessary
Uses final blends	**Process Focus**	
Uses suffixes correctly e.g., -s, -ing, -ed, -ly		
Uses syllables		
Uses editing skills		
	Correctly places quotation marks	
	Correctly places question marks	
	Correctly places apostrophes	
	Correctly places commas	
	Correctly divides story into paragraphs	
Publishes correct articles of work		
	Product Focus Varies sentence beginnings	
	Is able to sequence ideas	
	Uses a wide vocabulary	
	Writes in a variety of styles — friendly letter	
	— factual	
	— report	
	— imaginative	
	— retelling	
	— poetry	

Cumulative Record Card

(See page 28)

In written language, the cumulative record card would contain specific information gained from the data gathered. It is filled in at one month, six months, one year, and thereafter twice per year.

At one month, it would indicate the child's interest in writing and whether the early process skills are evident, and whether the child can recall the storyline.

At six months, and thereafter, it would indicate level of writing, attitudes, and skills.

Can the child write with confidence and enjoyment?

Can the child express himself or herself clearly in a written form?

What level of writing is the child at? (Emergent, Early, Fluency.)

Self-evaluation

Children need to play an active role in evaluation.

Self-evaluation can really only succeed where children have a chance to develop and improve their ideas about how to write by writing stories of many kinds, and teachers should aim to produce independent writers whose writing improves by writing.

The following are some suggestions to encourage self-evaluation:

Emergent/Early process skills:

— Focus the children on what they are able to do.
— Encourage them to think about what they could learn to do next.

Early/Fluency process skills:

— Encourage the child to self-edit.
— Encourage the child to fill in an individual "Skills I am able to do" chart in his or her personal writing book.

Early/Fluency process skills:

— Encourage children to make their own charts of stories they have written.
— Encourage children to make a comment on their stories. What did they like about the story? How could they improve it?

Children need to be made aware of what they are doing when they are writing and encouraged to analyze their own writing so that they may improve further.

52

"Skills I Am Able to Do" Charts

At the back of the child's written-language book paste "Look, I Can" or "Skills I am able to do" charts. After "conferencing" with the child, assist in filling in the checklist. Discuss with the child what he or she can do. Direct the child to think about what he or she needs to learn next.

Look, I Can									
Write letters									
Leave spaces									
Write the first letter in a word									
Write the last letter in a word									
Write some middle letters in a word									
Write some whole words									
Put a period and a capital letter in the right place									
Write one sentence									
Write two sentences									
Write three or more sentences									

Use at Emergent Level

Skills I Am Able to Do

Story Type

RP = Report	R = Retelling
I = Imaginative	D = Diary Writing
L = Letter	P = Poem

Type									
Use periods									
Use capital letter for beginning sentence									
Use capitals for names									
Use interesting sentence starters									
Recognize errors									
Correct spelling									
Use speech punctuation									
Use paragraphs									
Use "super" words									

Use at Early-Fluency Level

Date or color a square each time the child has successfully used the skill in his or her written work.

When the line is completely filled in, the child can be assured he or she has mastered that skill.

Under "Type" in "Skills I Am Able to Do", indicate the type of story the child has written. This will indicate whether the child is using a variety of genre.

Using the Data

The data collected is used in the following ways:

- Evaluating the program.
- Reporting to parents.

Evaluating the Program:

When evaluating the writing program in action, it is important to consider whether or not the teacher targets are being achieved.

— Is the program balanced?
— Are the children eager to write?
— Do the children demonstrate a real interest in the stories they have written and those of others?
— Is there evidence of emerging independence?
— Are children developing a wide vocabulary?
— Are the individual needs of each child being catered to?
— Is there time for them to practice their writing skills?

Reporting to Parents:

Reports should:
— Focus on the learning achievements of the individual child.
— Describe the knowledge, skills, attitudes, and values being developed.
— Be in sufficient detail for the parents to feel confident that the report informs them about the learning that has occurred.
— Be frequent and meaningful.
— Give opportunities for parents to share information about their child.

In reporting to parents on written language, the following specific suggestions are made:

1. Outline the writing program by newsletter or parent meeting. This could include the teacher targets and the methods by which the targets intend to be reached.

2. After one month of the school year, arrange a parent/teacher discussion. This is a time for the parents to share information about the child with the teacher. It would be important to find out the child's attitude toward written language at home; for example, whether the child is eager to write stories in spare time. The teacher might share with the parent the observation notes, samples of written language, and explain the child's stage of development and where he or she will be led to next. (It is important for parents to know where the children are going as well as where they've been and are right now.)

    Any relevant information resulting from this interview is recorded in the individual file or on the cumulative record card.

3. After approximately five months of the school year, a formal interview between parents and teacher is arranged. This is the time for the teacher to share with the parent the learning achievements of the child.

<u>The teacher will use the information gathered, e.g.:</u>

1. Observation notes
2. Written-language samples
3. Written-language checklists
4. "Skills I Am Able to Do" charts
5. Entry surveys

<u>At the conclusion of this interview, the parent should know specifically:</u>

— What the child is able to do in written language.
— What the next step(s) will be.
— The parental role in helping children achieve the next step(s).

At the conclusion of the school year, a written report is issued to parents. This should contain relevant, specific comments on the individual child's achievements. It should contain information as to the child's:

1. Understanding of writing.
2. Skills and knowledge of writing.
3. Attitudes toward written language.

(See Page 36 for a sample newsletter to parents.)

Spelling

Overview of the Instructional Year

Spelling is viewed in the context of writing rather than as an isolated skill.

Effective spelling instruction requires environments in which the children are encouraged to read and to write extensively.

The overview for spelling is divided into three stages: Emergent, Early, and Fluency.

Emergent means: The child is beginning to make a start.
Early means: The child is becoming aware of some conventional spellings.
Fluency means: The child is becoming independent

Overview of Spelling Program
Emergent Stage

Teacher's Targets and Method		Children's Targets	Monitoring
To model conventional spelling through class writing activities:	By modeling daily a story for children and focusing on the correct spelling of heavy-duty words.	To be able to write freely.	Observations.
To encourage and praise all spelling attempts:	By allowing children to write for themselves daily; by conferencing with children and checking off all correct letters or words.	To be able to write some words using the initial letter.	Identify children with speech problems (refer to speech therapist).
To teach children the names and sounds of alphabet letters:	By having children listen for initial sounds in reading and writing activities; by playing alphabet games; by having alphabet charts to refer to when writing.	To know letter names and sounds.	Monthly alphabet checks.
		To be able to spell correctly some heavy-duty words.	Written-language samples.
To make children aware of words that rhyme:	By using poems and songs and by involving children in rhyming activities.	To be able to distinguish between words that rhyme and words that don't.	Checklists.

Overview of Spelling Program
Early Stage

Teacher's Targets and Method	Children's Targets	Monitoring
To model conventional spelling through class writing activities: — By modeling daily a story for children, focusing on the correct spelling of heavy-duty words and some interest words.	To be able to write most words with the final letter correct.	Observations.
To encourage and praise all spelling attempts: — By allowing children to write for themselves daily; by conferencing with children and checking off all correct words.	To be able to use initial blends.	Written language samples to analyze spelling strategies.
To model skills and generalizations of spelling through class writing activities: — By focusing on end sounds, initial blends, and other generalizations that may be appropriate.	To be able to use vowels. / To be able to spell many heavy duty words correctly.	Weekly checking of individual writing – proof-reading and teacher checks.
To encourage children to proofread: — By having children underline approximations in their written work.	To develop a spelling conscience.	Checklists.
To encourage the use of dictionaries and other word sources to confirm spellings, or to correct approximations: — By helping children to use a dictionary, by playing dictionary games, and by providing a range of word resources to read and use in writing. By having words, words, words to read in the classroom.	To be able to underline approximations in written language.	
To encourage children to learn the conventional spelling of words they can almost spell: — By introducing an individual word card for words children have used in their own writing and can almost spell. By playing word games; by using the words in context.	To begin using word sources to correct approximations. / To begin to remember the correct spelling of some words.	

Overview of Spelling Program
Fluency Stage

Teacher's Targets and Method		Children's Targets	Monitoring
To model conventional spelling through class writing activities:	By modeling daily some writing for children, and focusing on the correct spelling of heavy-duty words and interest words.	To have a spelling conscience.	Observations.
To model skills and generalizations of spelling through class writing activities:	By focusing on final blends, suffixes, syllables and other generalizations.	To be able to proofread.	Written language samples to analyze spelling strategies.
To encourage and praise all spelling attempts:	By allowing children to write for themselves daily; by encouraging children to predict the most likely spelling; by conferencing.	To be able to use a dictionary correctly.	Weekly checklists of individual writing - proofreading and teacher checks.
To reinforce proofreading skills:	By encouraging children to underline approximations.	To be able to publish correct pieces of written work.	Checklists.
To reinforce the use of dictionaries and other word resources to confirm spellings, or to correct approximations:	By continuing to develop dictionary skills; by playing dictionary games; by providing a range of word resources to read and use in writing; by having many words to read in the classroom.	To have a large number of remembered spellings.	
To encourage children to learn the conventional spelling of words they can almost spell:	By continuing to develop an individual word card for words children have used in written language and can almost spell; by playing word games; by finding and using the words in context.	To be aware of spelling generalizations and use them correctly: e.g. final blends suffixes syllabification.	

An Explanation of Some Methods Mentioned in the Overview:

Daily Modeling:
  The teacher writes a story for the children. Use this time to focus children on spelling conventions.

Emergent level:
  What sound can you hear at the beginning of ...?
  Who can write it?
  Who knows how to spell this word?
  Write it in the air.
  Find it in the room.

Early level:
  What sound can you hear at the end of this word?
  What blend does this word start with?
  What letter(s) come in the middle of the word?
  I have spelled a word wrong in my story. Who can find it? How will I fix it?

Fluency level:
  What blend can you hear at the end of this word?
  What ending will I put on this word?
  What do I have to remember to do?
  How can I break the word up into syllables or clusters of sounds to help me spell it?
  If I have made spelling mistakes in my story, how can I check them?

Rhyming Activities:

Through poetry and song, get the children to listen for words that rhyme.

Make them aware of the parts of rhyming words that are the same and parts that are different.

High-Interest and High-Frequency Words:

Use every opportunity to write words in the classroom:

— Captions on artwork.
— Captions on science exhibits.
— Labels.
— Lists of words about the current theme.
— Lists of words "we can nearly spell." (Emergent, Early levels)

Proof reading:

Early-Fluency level:

— Encourage the children to read and reread their stories looking for words they think they might have spelled incorrectly.
— Encourage them to underline their errors.
— Encourage them to use a dictionary or other word sources around the room to correct the error, above their approximation. (The approximation should not be erased on the draft writing.) By leaving the approximation, the teacher can see just what the child is able to do. It can also provide a teaching point.

Using Dictionaries:

Early level:

1. Use the alphabet chart to begin early dictionary skills. For example, focus children on:

— What letter comes after *b* ?
— What is the first letter in the alphabet?
— What is the last letter in the alphabet?
— What letter comes before *m* ?
— What letter comes between *c* and *e* ?

2. Introduce children to dictionaries:

— Turn to the first half.
— Turn to the last half.
— Turn to the middle.
— Practice finding words.

Fluency level:

Make children very familiar with the dictionary.
Practice finding words quickly.
Play alphabetical-order games.

Teaching Names and Sounds of the Alphabet:

<u>Emergent level:</u>
  Teach and reinforce sounds of the alphabet in all reading and writing activities.
  Have an alphabet chart—refer to it when writing.
  Share alphabet books.
  Make individual alphabet books.
  Play alphabet games (I Spy).
  Play games to find a special focus letter per week that the children find in all reading and writing activities. Relate learning to context.
  Use the focus letter as the handwriting instruction for the week.

"Conferencing" with Children:

<u>Emergent:</u>
  Check and praise all correct letters and words.

<u>Early:</u>
  Check and praise all correct letters and words.
  Praise all attempts to underline approximations.
  Praise all attempts to correct approximations.

<u>Fluency:</u>
  Praise all attempts to correct approximations.

Note: The teacher accepts the child's effort at all stages but must ensure that a correct model is provided.

1. At the Emergent level, the teacher models the child's story underneath the child's attempts.

2. At the Early level, when many words are being spelled correctly, the child skips a line in writing so that the correct spelling can easily be inserted.

3. At the Fluency level, the correct spelling is placed above the approximations, mostly by the child when editing.

Individual Word Cards

At the early stage of spelling, when the child is able to spell many heavy-duty, or high frequency words correctly, an individual word card can be introduced.

Aa	Bb	Cc	Dd	Ee	Ff	Gg	Hh

On this card put heavy-duty words the child can almost spell. These words are taken from his or her personal writing.

For example, Adam at the Early stage of writing wrote *fond* for *found*. He could almost spell that word but now needed to focus on its conventional spelling.

This word could be placed on Adam's card. It is not necessary to place a word on the card each time he writes, only those words he can almost spell should be entered.

If Adam uses that word again in his writing, he can refer to his individual word card to confirm his spelling.

He now knows there is a correct way to spell the word, and by writing it in its conventional way, he is reinforcing that spelling.

These word cards can be taken home to parents with a covering letter outlining the spelling program.

Monitoring Progress

In spelling, the following methods are used in monitoring:

Emergent Monitoring	Early Monitoring	Fluency Monitoring
Observations	Observations	Observations
Identify children with speech problems (refer to speech therapist)	Written language samples to analyze spelling strategies	Written language samples to analyze spelling strategies
Monthly alphabet checks	Weekly checking of individual writing—proof reading and teacher checks	Weekly checking of individual writing—proof reading and teacher checks
Written language samples		
Checklists	Checklists	Checklists

Observations of Spelling

It is important to observe children's spelling and the strategies they use, and to be aware of their attitude towards spelling. The following observations can be made:

All levels:
- Is the child confident about attempting to write words he or she may not know how to spell?
- Is the child only writing words he or she knows how to spell?
- Is the child interested in words?
- Is the child using his or her knowledge of spelling?

Early-Fluency Level:
- Is the child developing a spelling conscience?
- Is the child eager and willing to proof read?
- Is the child remembering conventional spellings?
- Is the child confident about his or her ability to spell?
- Is the child able to make generalizations quickly?

Generalizations:

It is important to introduce and reinforce spelling generalizations through reading and writing activities—Shared book, Guided reading, and modeling as examples.

Generalizations to introduce or reinforce when appropriate are:

*   visual and auditory identification of the initial consonants, initial blends, final consonants, final blends.
*   recognition of vowel symbols.
*   suffixes.
*   syllabification of words.
*   capital letters for names and proper nouns.
*   contractions e.g. I'll...
*   simple conventions, such as 'q' is followed by 'u'.
*   words with similar spelling patterns.

Children with Speech Problems

Notes need to be made on the spelling cumulative record card if a speech problem is apparent. Speech problems can hinder spelling development. (Note hearing and sight difficulties as well.)

The particular sounds causing concern should be noted. The parents should be encouraged to help overcome the problem. If the case is severe, the speech therapist will need to be advised.

Monthly Alphabet Checks—Emergent Level:

Making a regular check on the child's letter/sound knowledge helps the teacher know what the child should be using in his or her written language. Many at the Emergent level have a sound knowledge of the alphabet but do not use it in their written language. They need to be encouraged to do so. (Note letter knowledge is closely related to reading progress as well.)

Written-language Samples

These written-language samples taken six times per year indicate the spelling stage of the child, what his or her needs are, and whether progress is evident. Notes are made on the samples concerning both the written language and spelling development.

Written-language samples showing spelling progressions:

Emergent

I WT to the
b9. I W f
A WK.

I went to the
beach. I went for
a walk.   Adam

Writing freely.
Knows letter names and
sounds.
Writing words with correct
initial letter.
Writing some heavy-duty
words.

Early

I went   to   John's
house
hose.   We   Playd   on
                played
the   traPlen.
           trampoline   Adam

Using vowels, blends.
Writing most words with final
letter correct.
Writing many heavy-duty words
correctly.
Begin an individual word card
for heavy-duty words almost
correct, e.g., *house, played.*

Fluency

Grandma and Grandpa

Last night I went to Grandma's and Grandpa's. I had angel food cake. then I played with the dogs. I thro the ball
threw

down stes and they
stairs

Cath it.
caught

Locating approximations. Using a dictionary or other resource means to correct approximations.

Spelling Checklists

The checklists are a means of checking and recording what the child has attained.

These should be filled in, in conjunction with the writing checklists.

Record of Written Language and Spelling Development

Spelling Stage 1 Emergent	Written language Stage 1 Emergent	Date when mastered — Comment if necessary
	Process Focus	
	Pre-letter writing	
	Writing letters	
	Correct directional movement	
	Leaves spaces	
	Uses approximations	
	Uses initial consonants	
Knows letter names and letter sounds		
	Uses some known words in correct places	
	Product Focus Able to select own topic to write on.	

Record of Written Language Development and Spelling Development

Spelling Stage 2 Early	Written Language Stage 2 Early	Date when mastered - Comment if necesary
Process Focus Uses end sounds of most words correctly		
Uses vowels		
Able to spell many heavy-duty words correctly		
Uses more correct spellings than approximations		
Uses initial blends		
Uses editing skills: Underlines approximations		
Uses word sources to correct approximations		
	Uses periods in correct place	
	Uses full stops in correct place	
	Product Focus Writes a title	
	Varies topic choice	

Record of Written Language and Spelling Development

Spelling Stage 3 Fluency	Written Language Stage 3 Fluency	Date when mastered - Comment if necessary
Uses final blends Uses suffixes correctly e.g., -s, -ing, -ed, -ly Uses syllables	**Process Focus**	
Uses editing skills		
	Correctly places quotation marks	
	Correctly places question marks	
	Correctly places apostrophes	
	Correctly places commas	
	Correctly divides story into paragraphs	
Publishes correct articles of work		
	Product Focus Varies sentence beginnings	
	Is able to sequence ideas	
	Uses a wide vocabulary	
	Writes in a variety of styles — friendly letter	
	— factual	
	— report	
	— imaginative	
	— retelling	
	— poetry	

Self-evaluation:

Children need to play an active role in evaluation.

Self-evaluation can really only succeed where children have a chance to develop and improve their ideas about how to spell by spelling many words.

Teachers should aim to produce independent spellers whose spelling improves by writing words. Spelling and writing progress (and reading as well) is closely related.

The following are some suggestions to encourage self-evaluation:

Emergent/Early Levels:

1. Focus the child on what he or she knows.
2. Encourage the child to use what he or she knows.
3. Be positive toward all spelling attempts made by the child.

Early/Fluency Levels:

1. Be positive toward all spelling attempts made.
2. Encourage the child to check his or her own work, to check off correctly spelled words, and to underline those words that he or she thinks are not correctly spelled.
3. Encourage the child to correct errors.
4. Encourage the child to compare how he or she spelled the word to the conventional spelling.
5. Encourage the child to make a spelling list of words he or she should know how to spell.
6. Encourage the child to take an interest in words.

A child should develop a spelling conscience and be aware of how he or she can be responsible for his or her own spelling development.

Using the Data:

The data collected is used in the following ways:

- Evaluating the program
- Reporting to parents

Evaluating the program:

When evaluating the spelling program, it is important to consider whether or not the teacher targets are being achieved:

Is the program purposeful?
Are the children aware of conventional spellings?
Are the children being encouraged to attempt to spell all words?
Are the children developing a spelling conscience?
Is there an awareness of precision? (The whole process is one of increasing precision.)
Are they enjoying looking at words and saying them?
Do they have a sound alphabet knowledge?
Are the individual needs of each child being catered to?
Is there time for them to practice their spelling skills?

Reporting to Parents

The same guidelines as established for reading and written language should be followed for spelling.

1. Outline by newsletter or parent meeting the spelling program. This could include the teacher targets and methods by which these targets intend to be reached. It should be made very clear to parents the importance of allowing a child to approximate a word.

2. At one month, parent/teacher discussions. A parent sharing time. The teacher could perhaps give the parent some positive ideas of how to encourage a spelling awareness.

3. At five months, or thereabouts, at a formal interview. The teacher should share with the parents the learning achievements of the child. The teacher will use the data gathered:

— Monthly alphabet checks: Emergent level—indicate to the parents the letter/sound knowledge of the child. Suggest positive ways the parents can assist in developing this further, if necessary.
— Written-language samples — share these samples with the parents and indicate the child's spelling stage.
— Written-language and spelling-development checklists: Share these with the parents.

<u>At the conclusion of this interview, the parents should know specifically:</u>

— What the child's spelling stage is.
— What the next stage should be.
— How parents can help in their child's spelling development.

4. At the conclusion of the school year, a written report is issued to parents:
   This should contain relevant, specific comments on the individual child's achievements. It should contain information as to the child's skills and knowledge of spelling and attitudes toward spelling.

Sample of a Newsletter to Parents:

Dear Parents,

Your child is ready to begin looking carefully at the spelling of some words.

These will be words your child has used in his or her personal writing. They will be words your child can almost spell.

Your child may wish to share these words with you. If so, he or she will bring home an individual word card. The following are some suggestions for you to help with the retention of these spelling conventions.

Your child can:
— Find these words in newspapers or magazines.
— Cut the letters out and rearrange in the correct order.
— Use metallic letters to make the words on the refrigerator or some other place.
— Play word games such as Scrabble ®.
— Write the words using many different media, e.g., thick pens, thin pens, sand, paint.

It is not intended that you should drill or test your child on each word, but rather make the retention of conventional forms of spelling a "fun" experience.

Yours sincerely,

Monitoring Timetable

In the introduction of this book, it was stated that monitoring should be ongoing and an integral part of the class program.

To assist teachers in making this possible, a monitoring timetable has been devised.

Establishing a monitoring timetable means that the teacher needs only to focus on one area to be monitored each week. Naturally, there are some areas that require ongoing monitoring. They cannot simply be slotted into a weekly timeslot.

The timetable is organized into an eight-week block. After eight weeks, the timetable is repeated. It should be emphasized that the areas to be monitored form part of the normal class program. As one example, written-language samples should be taken as part of the written-language program, and running records should be taken in reading time.

Running Records have been given a two-week time slot to ensure that the teacher has time to monitor each child.

Observation of children is given a two-week time slot because it is considered important that the teacher takes time to observe and focus closely on individual children's attitudes and interest in reading and writing, but other observations are naturally ongoing. The following is an example of a Monitoring Timetable.

Monitoring Timetable

Week	Methods of Data Gathering	Ongoing Data Gathering
1	Observation of children	Entry survey (5-year-old children after one week at school)
2	Observation of children	
3	Running records; fill in reading checklist	Emergent check (reading)
4	Running records; fill in reading checklist	Diagnostic surveys (after one year)
5	Written-language sample; fill in checklists	
6	Handwriting sample; sample or letter formation check	Alphabet check (Emergent level)
7	Running records; fill in reading checklist	Cumulative record entries: 1 month, 6 months, 1 year
8	Running records; fill in reading checklist	Observations

Conclusion:

As teachers it is our aim to provide a happy, caring environment, with all children actively involved in the learning process.

This requires thoughtful planning and careful monitoring and evaluating. It requires not only evaluating the children, but continually evaluating our own understanding of how our particular children learn, what we are presenting to them, whether we are encouraging independence, and whether we are providing the facilities, materials, and opportunities for the child to learn successfully.

Suggested References

For further information on the techniques of taking running records, see:

Clay, Marie. *The Early Detection of Reading Difficulties.* Published by Heinemann in 1979.

For information on taking a diagnostic survey, see:

Clay, Marie. *The Early Detection of Reading Difficulties.* Published by Heinemann, 1979.

For information on the features of the three stages of reading - Emergent, Early, Fluency, see:

Cutting, Brian. *Getting Started in Whole Language.* Published by Wendy Pye Ltd, 1989, and distributed in the USA by The Wright Group.

For information on the approaches used in the teaching of reading, see:

Cutting, Brian. *Sunshine in the Classroom (Books One and Two).* Published by Wendy Pye Ltd, 1988. See also, *Getting Started in Whole Language.*

Useful information can also be found in:

Clay, Marie. *What Did I Write.* Heinemann, 1975.

Goodman, Ken et al (Eds). *The Whole-Language Evaluation Book.* Heinemann, 1989.

Notes

Notes

Notes